Just to say
Thank You . . .

To: Dr. Jean Melvin-Martin
From: Rev. Louis & Sis. Dianne Ridgley
Oct. 9, 2004

Just to say
Thank You ...

p

This is a Parragon Publishing Book
This edition published in 2003

Parragon Publishing
Queen Street House
4 Queen Street
Bath BA1 1HE, UK

This book was created by Magpie Books,
an imprint of Constable & Robinson Ltd.

Designed by Tony and Penny Mills

A copy of the British Library Cataloguing-in-Publication Data
is available from the British Library

Printed in Italy

ISBN 1-84273-527-6

INTRODUCTION

The ability to understand and appreciate the kindness of those around us and to know the meaning of gratitude is one of the most important things that distinguishes human beings from other species.

Whether it is a stranger in the street who has cheered us on our way; a neighbour or colleague who has given us a meal, or the enduring kindness of old friends and close family, the world is filled with people to whom we owe a big debt of gratitude and to whom we can wholeheartedly offer a deep and sincere "Thank You" for making our lives happier and richer.

Let us be grateful to people who make us happy; they are the charming gardeners who make our souls blossom.

MARCEL PROUST

Do not complain that there are thorns on roses. Be thankful there are roses on thorns.

HENRY WARD BEECHER
(1813—1887)

Would that this garland fair
Might weave around thy life
A spell to shield from care
A guard from every strife

ANON
(19th century)

Blessed are those that can give without
remembering and receive without forgetting.
ANON

Gratitude is not only the greatest of virtues,
but the parent of all the others.
CICERO

II

I thank God more for friends than for my daily
bread—for friendship is the bread of
my heart.

MARY MITFORD
(1787—1855)

You have particular reason to place confidence
in those who have shown affection for you in
your early days, when you were incapable of
making them any return.

LORD CHESTERFIELD
Principles of Politeness and of
Knowing the World
(1886)

BASKET OF APPLES
Come, come my beloved
And sympathize with me
Receive the little basket
And the blessing so free
ANON
Note from a 19th-century Shaker woman

Nothing is more honorable than
a grateful heart.
SENECA
(d. AD 65)

I had many presents, but I liked best
the portrait of my mother, whom I
scarcely remember, which my
grandfather brought me.

Written and illustrated by
RANDOLPH CALDECOTT
(1846—1886)

From too much love of living,
From hope and fear set free,
We thank with brief thanksgiving
Whatever gods may be.

ALGERNON SWINBURNE
(1837—1909)

O Lord, that lends me life,
Lend me a heart replete with thankfulness!

WILLIAM SHAKESPEARE,
(1564—1616)

Gratitude is the fairest blossom which
springs from the soul.

HENRY WARD BEECHER
(1813—1887)

For truly, the greatest of all external blessings is it to be able to lean your heart against another heart, faithful, tender, true, and tried, and record with a thankfulness that years deepen instead of diminishing, "I have got a friend!"

DINAH MARIA MULOCK CRAIK
(1826—1887)

Gratitude is a fruit of great cultivation; you do not find it among gross people.

SAMUEL JOHNSON
(1785)

But when O Wells! thy
roses came to me,
My sense with their deli-
ciousness was spelled:
Soft voices had they, that
with tender plea
Whispered of peace, and
truth, and friendliness
unquelled.

JOHN KEATS
(1785—1821)
to a friend

Swift gratitude is sweetest; if it
delays, all gratitude is empty—
unworthy of the name.

ANON

From long practice, she does it a
hundred times better than I
could do; nay, even takes a plea-
sure and pride in it, for which I
am truly thankful, and sincerely
indebted to her, too: for a good
cook is a household blessing, and
no small contributor to health,
temper, and enjoyment.

DINAH MARIA MULOCK CRAIK
(1826—1887)

GRATITUDE

Everytime I walk through my garden in fall I utter up a quiet prayer of thanksgiving to God who has given me so much to enjoy throughout the year.

When I pause by my small bed of herbs, parsley, thyme, sage, rosemary, and a small bay tree in an old clay pot, I think how wonderful it is that each of these is so beautiful to look at, so rich in flavor and bouquet, and yet each is so completely different from its companion.

I love the smell of the mown grass when I make my final cut before the winter; I love the feel of the warm soil as I take up my summer tubers to store away for next year and, as I gather the last few roses of the year, the memory of their heavy scent and the perfection of their multi-colored petals through the whole long summer overwhelms me.

I store away my apples for the winter and as I order them on their trays I notice the subtle variations of color and pattern on each one. It is still amazing to me to think how the small pink and white blossom of the spring has been transmuted by the warmth and light of the sun into a thing of such individual perfection.

When I look up at the infinite depth of space with its countless stars and galaxies and I think of the perfection of even the smallest part of Creation I find I am quite unable to express my amazement that I can have been given so much to see and to enjoy.

GEORGE ROGERS

It is therefore recommended ... to set apart Thursday the eighteenth day of December next, for solemn thanksgiving and praise, that with one heart and one voice the good people may express the grateful feelings of their hearts and consecrate themselves to the service of their divine benefactor ...

SAMUEL ADAMS,
Father of the American Revolution, on
November 1, 1777
adopted by the 13 states as the first
official Thanksgiving Proclamation.

What sunshine is to flowers, smiles are to humanity.

These are but trifles, to be sure; but, scattered along life's pathway, the good they do is inconceivable.

JOSEPH ADDISON
(1672—1719)

Friend of my life! My ardent spirit burns,
And all the tribute of my heart returns,
For boons accorded, goodness ever new,
The gifts still dearer, as the giver you.

ROBERT BURNS
(1759—1796)

Dear good friend, the safety pin is a duck,
a 1,000 thanks.

AUBREY BEARDSLEY,
to his publisher
(1897)

That thrill of thankful gladness [is] oftenest caused by little things—a lovely bit of nature, a holiday after long toil, a sudden piece of good news, an unexpected face, or a letter that warms one's inmost heart.

DINAH MARIA MULOCK CRAIK

(1826—1887)

A Woman's Thoughts About Women

Ah, God! A poor soul can but thank Thee
For such a delectable day!

CHARLES KINGSLEY

(1819—1875)

Thank you five hundred and forty times for the exquisite piece of workmanship which was brought into the room this morning, while we were at breakfast.

JANE AUSTEN,
to her sister
(1813)

Beggar that I am,
I am even poor in thanks.
WILLIAM SHAKESPEARE
(1564—1616)

A thousand thanks, my dear, for my waistcoat, which I wore the last time I dined at the Hall, to the great admiration of the ladies. It is perfectly genteel and elegant.

WILLIAM COWPER,
to his cousin
(1787)

And though I ebb in worth
I'll flow in thanks.
JOHN TAYLOR
(1580—1653)

Being an old aunt does bring its problems. I am very grateful to my nephews and nieces who remember me each year and think of a present suitable for a person such as myself, but I now have sufficient trifles in my sewing box to darn and make good for the next thousand years.

EDITH SOMERS,
to an old friend
(1873)

I am of the opinion, in which I am every day confirmed by observation, that gratitude is one of those things that cannot be bought. It must be with you when you are born, or else all the obligations in the world will not create it. An outward show may be made to satisfy decency, and to prevent reproach; but a real sense of a kind thing is a gift of nature, and never was, nor can be acquired.

LORD HALIFAX

(1633–1695)

How wonderful it would be if we could help our children and grandchildren to learn thanksgiving at an early age.

Learning to say thank you opens doors within the mind to a whole new world of perception. It changes our whole personality. We can be resentful, negative—or thankful. Thankful people want to give, they radiate happiness, they are a lodestar to all around them, who are enriched by their company.

FREDERICK SMALL

Thanks to God who giveth meat
Convenient unto all to eat:
Thanks for tea and buttered toast,
Father, Son, and Holy Ghost.

RICHARD LAWSON GALES (adapted)
(1862—1927)

The Duke is very sensible of Miss J.'s offer of service in case the Duke should be sick or afflicted. The Duke is much obliged to her. He is quite well. He has no reason to believe that he will have occasion to trouble her upon any object whatever.

DUKE OF WELLINGTON,
to a persistent female admirer
(1840)

I thank the goodness and the grace
  Which on my birth have smiled,
And made me, in these infant days
  A happy little child.
     JANE TAYLOR (adapted)
      (1783—1824)

Now when the senses dim,
But now from the heart of joy,
I would remember Him:
Take the thanks of a boy.
   HENRY CHARLES BEECHING
    (1859—1919)
     Prayer at Even

I beg to acknowledge the receipt of your letter, officially informing me that the Committee award me a second-class gold medal. Pray convey my sentiments of tempered and respectable joy to the gentlemen of the Committee, and my complete appreciation of the second-hand compliment paid me.

J. MCNEILL WHISTLER

(1834—1903)

Thank you, pretty cow, that made
Pleasant milk to soak my bread,
Every day and every night,
Warm, and fresh, and sweet,
    and white.
    ANN TAYLOR (1783—1824)
    and JANE TAYLOR (1782—1866)

When you are gone I find your flowers ... thank you. Count among the miracles that your flowers live with me—I accept that for an omen, dear—dearest! Flowers in general, all other flowers, die of despair.

ELIZABETH BARRETT,
to her future husband
(1845)

Thanks for your nice little note, though I am sorry to hear you find Through the Looking-glass so uninteresting. You see I have done my best, so it isn't really my fault if you think Tweedledum and Tweedledee stupid, and wish that I had left out all about the train and the gnat.

LEWIS CARROLL,

to a child

(c. 1880)

44

I have received the splendid dates you sent,
and they now rival in my affections my figs
and mushrooms.

PLINY THE YOUNGER

(62 to c. AD 105)

Oh! Sir, I shall take care how I ever ask favours of you again! ... It would have been unpleasant enough to be refused; but to obtain more than one asked is the most provoking thing in the world!

HORACE WALPOLE

(1717—1797)

A wagging tail is more sincere
than any thank-you letter.
ANONYMOUS DOG-LOVER

Feeling gratitude and not expressing it is like
wrapping a gift and not giving it.
JOHN GREENLEAF WHITTIER
(1807—1892)

Cats have a far stronger sense of obligation than any other animal. Horses don't bring their rider a mouthful of thistles and dogs don't produce a succulent bone they have allowed to ripen in the garden for the last six months. Cats, though, produce a small bird on the dining room table or a pair of rabbit legs with fur left on to give a richer texture and then wait eagerly to see you munch it down and show appreciation of their kindness.

JANET MORRIS

What moistens the lip and what
   brightens the eye?
What calls back the past, like the
   rich pumpkin pie ...
Then thanks for thy present!
   None sweeter or better
E'er smoked from an oven or
   circled a platter!

JOHN GREENLEAF WHITTIER
(1807—1892)

I give thee thanks for the beauty of colours, for the harmony of sounds, for the pleasantness of odours.

THOMAS TRAHERNE

(1636—1674)

Do we want our homes to be happy? If we do, let them be the abiding place of prayer, thanksgiving and gratitude.

GEORGE ALBERT SMITH

To receive a present handsomely and in a right
spirit, even when you have none to give in
return, is to give one in return.

LEIGH HUNT
(1784—1859)

He who receives a good turn, should never
forget it: he who does one, should never
remember it.

ANON

THANK YOU LETTERS

Don't make the children say things they do not want to. Protect them from the petty insincerities of social life as long as possible.

LILLIAN EICHLER

Book of Etiquette

(1922)

Never accept of favours and hospitatilites without rendering in exchange of civilities when opportunity offers.

THOMAS E. HILL

Hill's Manual

(1885)

Though small the gift to thee I send
Acceptance let it meet
For even trifles from a friend
In friendship's eyes are sweet.

ANON

from a 19th-century
friendship album

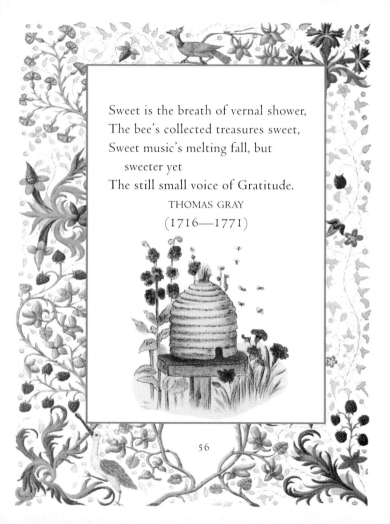

Sweet is the breath of vernal shower,
The bee's collected treasures sweet,
Sweet music's melting fall, but
    sweeter yet
The still small voice of Gratitude.

THOMAS GRAY
(1716—1771)

It is not enough to dine and breakfast at people's houses; you ought to visit them often, and prove to them, that it is not their kitchen alone, which draws you to their houses ... When politeness might not dictate a visit of this description, gratitude will teach it you as a duty. It is the very least one can do to thank the person who has been instrumental to your passing an agreeable day, by causing you to make an excellent dinner with him.

DICK HUMELBERGIUS SECUNDUS

Apician Morsels

(1829)

Thanks in old age—thanks ere I go,
For health, the midday sun, the impalpable air
    —for life, mere life,
For precious ever-lingering
    memories, (of you my mother dear—you,
    father—you, brothers, sisters, friends,)
For all my days ...

WALT WHITMAN
(1819—1891)

Thank you for writing to me frequently, the one way in which you can make your presence felt, for I never have a letter from you without immediately feeling we are together.

SENECA

(4 BC—AD 65)

Gratitude is a very pleasant sensation, both for those who feel and to those who excite it. No one who confers a favour can say with *truth* that they "want no thanks". They always do.

MISS LESLIE

The Behaviour Book: A Manual for Ladies

(1853)

Gratitude is the memory of the heart.

JEAN BAPTISTE MASSIEU

(*c.* 1800)

Glory be to God for dappled things—
For skies of couple-colour as a brindled
     cow;
For rose-moles all in stipple upon trout
     that swim;
Fresh-firecoal chestnut-falls; finches'
     wings;
Landscape plotted and pieced—fold, fallow
     and plough;
And all trades, their gear and tackle and
     trim ...

GERARD MANLEY HOPKINS
(1844—1889)

O Lord, that lends me life,
Lend me a heart replete with thankfulness!

WILLIAM SHAKESPEARE

(1564—1616)

Lord, Thou has given me a cell
    Wherein to dwell;
A little house, whose humble roof
    Is weather-proof …
Thou mak'st my teeming hen to lay
    Her egg each day …
All these, and better, Thou dost send
    Me, to this end,
That I should render, for my part,
    A thankful heart.

ROBERT HERRICK

(1591—1674)

Acknowledgements

Jacket picture A Penny for Yourself, c. 1870 (w/c) by James Clarke Waite (fl. 1863—85). John Noot Galleries, Broadway, Worcestershire, UK/Bridgeman Art Library.

page 11 Girl Making a Bouquet of Flowers, 1849 (oil on canvas) by Augustus Egg (1816—63). Harris Museum and Art Gallery, Preston, Lancashire, UK/Bridgeman Art Library.

page 14 A Boy Bringing Pomegranates, c.1662 by Pieter de Hooch (1629—84). Wallace Collection, London, UK/Bridgeman Art Library.

page 19 The Love Token, 1888 (panel) by Albert Friedrich Schroder (b.1854). Bonhams, London, UK/Bridgeman Art Library

page 29 The Letter (oil on canvas) by Tito Conti (1842—1924). Private Collection/Bonhams, London, UK/Bridgeman Art Library.

page 31 The Hard Working Mother, 1740 by Jean-Baptiste Simeon Chardin (1699—1779). Louvre, Paris, France/Peter Willi/Bridgeman Art Library.

page 39 Convalescent (oil on panel) by Charles West Cope (1811—90) Mallett & Son Antiques Ltd., London, UK/Bridgeman Art Library.

page 42 Portrait of Mlle de Rohan (oil on canvas) by Alfred Emile Stevens (1803—1906). South African National Gallery, Cape Town, South Africa/Bridgeman Art Library.

page 51 The Priest's Birthday (detail) by V. Chevilliard (1841—1904). Josef Mensing Gallery, Hamm-Rhynern, Germany/Bridgeman Art Library.

page 61 Day Dreams by Alfred Walter Bayes (1858—1903). York City Art Gallery, North Yorkshire, UK/Bridgeman Art Library.

The pictures on pages 46, 47, 48, and 54 are courtesy of Celia Haddon. All other pictures are from a private collection.